TRAVELERS

TRAVELERS

POEMS

CURT G. CURTIN

Copyright © 2025 by Curt G. Curtin.

Cover photo by Clair Degutis, Princeton, MA

All rights reserved. No part of this publication may be reproduced, distributed, or transmitted in any form or by any electronic or mechanical means, including information storage and retrieval systems, without a prior written permission from the publisher, except by reviewers, who may quote brief passages in a review, and certain other noncommercial uses permitted by the copyright law.

Library of Congress Control Number: 2025902297

ISBN: 979-8-89228-431-8   (Paperback)
ISBN: 979-8-89228-432-5   (eBook)

Book Ordering Information:
Atticus Publishing
548 Market St PMB 70756
San Francisco, CA 94104
(888) 208-9296
info@atticuspublishing.com
www.atticuspublishing.com

Printed in the United States of America

ACKNOWLEDGEMENTS

"Grief," "Family" and "Cemetery Stones in Winter" were published in <u>The Black River: Death Poems</u>. Deirdre Pulgram-Arthen, Ed. Northfield, MA: NatureCulture, LLC, 2024.

"Suis Generis" won first prize in the Women's Week Poetry Invitational, Westfield State University, and was published in a broadside for that occasion, 1985.

"The Castle Pub," and "Penelope" first appeared in the author's chapbook, <u>Pacing the Floor</u>, 1979. "The Castle Pub," was recorded by Curt Curtin on Themes and Variations, Texas Public Radio, Treehouse Productions.

"Familiar Lines" was first published in <u>Kerry Dancers</u>, Kelsay Books, 2020.

"The Poet Donates His Body to a Medical School" was first published in <u>For Arts' Sake</u>, Kelsay Books, 2019. That collection, with the poem bookmarked, traveled with Curt's body when it was donated to the anatomical gift program at the University of Massachusetts Medical School in August 2024.

CONTENTS

ARRIVALS

Tribal History	3
Layers	4
Harmattan	5
West Africa	6
Hounde	11
Under ground	13
Just This	14
City Garden	15
Asian Maple in a Clay Pot	16
Within	17
Riding the Boston "T"	18
The Shaper	19
The Dance	20
Inscape	21
Life Without Intention	22
On the Work of Purposes	23
In the Swing of the Sea	24
Stone Dream	25
Breaking (or fractal form)	26
Clouds	27
In-stress	28
Quiet Lives	29
The Castle Pub, Edinburgh	30
Grounds	34
Octobre dans Le Parc Gatineau	35
Snowfall	36
Sunset, December 31	37

THE WOMEN

Exegesis (Genesis 3, 6) 41
Woman 42
African Emanation 43
Stranger 44
All that's best of dark and bright* 45
Dance 46
Among the Unclean 47
Dreamscape 48
Ice 49
Mirror Mirror 51
Undertow 52
Venus 53
Summa 54
Refrain 55
Sui Generis 56
Holding the Door 59
Penelope 60
The Thorn Speaks to Sleeping Beauty 61
Decision 62
Genesis 63

BOYS AND MEN

Boy With A Long-stemmed Rose 67
Consummation 68
Familiar Lines 69
Little Red Riding Hood and the Real Wolf 70
Building Wall 71
Work 72
Old (Black) Joe 73
Haiku -- New Orleans, 2005 75
Sea-change 76

The Inmate 77
By the Rude Bridge 78
Paralysis 79
Men Have Closets, Too 80
Chemistry 81
Science Friction 82
I Robot 83
Singularity: an Experiment with a Man-child 84
Stranger 86

DEPARTURES

Flood's Dream 89
Survival 90
Relation 91
Awe 92
Perspective 93
The Wizard's Book 94
Song 95
…reason is but choosing * 96
Paradox 97
In His Eighty-first Year 98
November of An Old Professor 99
Grief 100
Cemetery Stones in Winter 101
Family 102
Conversation 104
Burial Day 105
Cemetery Stones 106
Forest Hills Cemetery 107
In a Graveyard 109
Old Men on Monday 110
Oh, Them Golden Years 111
The New Old Old 112

Lucinda	113
Naming in the Wards	114
On Becoming Blind	115
Johnny Lost His "Mister"	116
Dementia	117
Places in the Heart*	118
The Poet Donates His Body to a Medical School	119
Le Chaim	120

ARRIVALS

Tribal History

The tribes of humankind teach design.
They call it *holy word* from visions made
in early history, from sand to sacred sites.
What lucky minds to land upon that spot
and make it yield, not a crop, but eternity.

(Oh, how I wish to ask a Bangladeshi farmer
what she thinks of that.)

Layers

Saharan desert, vast and arid, wind, grit
and abrasion; east from the Atlantic
to the Nile, south from the Atlas Mountains
through purgatorial Sahel, creeping lethal
into green—*so fell the eternal heat, by which
the sand was kindled, like tinder under
flint and steel*--myth of desolation mocked
by beautiful design, color and line of lions.

Who wanders here sees shimmering heat,
demon dreams, imagines sulphurous fire
under massive plates, waiting angels.
These avow one holy rock beneath.
and pray the subjugation of sand, their
lack of traction psychical surrender.

Pray heed the evidence of sediments,
the measure of generations, wanderers
long before eternity became an arid place.

So fell ... steel. Dante's Inferno, Canto XIV,
Translation, Carlyle-Wicksteed.

Harmattan

Another wind across Sahara whirls
Grit sticks under eyelids, TV screens,
corporate ledgers, western dreams.
Harama, Haram
The wind speaks: *harama*, you shall
not thirst for other wells; *haram*,
there is evil worse than thirst; there
is evil worse than death. Your death
brings life to righteousness.
Harama: Dust to dust,
season of dust in infidel's eyes.

Arabic: *harama*--to prohibit; *haram*--evil things, teachings
Harmattan: dry, dusty wind. In season, it blows along northwest Africa to the Sahel.

West Africa

Ouagadougou

Army at the airport, not mine,
haughty not quite angry seems,
seems I may not stride up white
American to say—as if expecting
service tout-de-suite Monsieur,
my baggage did not get here from Dakar.
I learn that soldiers in Burkina Faso
do not think Americans are kings.

Buzzards waddle dirt streets at dawn,
beautiful African sunrise stridesrdry heat in season Harmattan,
Harmattan, when air is choked with grit,
eyelashes stuck with rusty dust
on wind that rides Sahara's advancing tide.

Tu Babu,
too hot for you?

Everybody everyday go to Le Marche,
field of many tents and corrugated tin,
and if you look at anything too long
a quick tenacious seller pulls you in--
too late to slip away, the bargaining begins.
Every day bargain day, rhythm of Marche;
"Why buy your dolo, why buy rice? I
can live on toh." "Oh? Where's your pride?"
Deep inside, every bargain day. "Hey,
I don't care for Bata shoe." "No?
Better than a mamba bite your toe."

Rhythm of Marche.
Peanut butter tubs, pick a live chicken,
spice piled high, rice loose to scoop,
red-orange-black-blue-yellow cloth,
good enough to please French gouverners,
good enough to please Belgian king;
come monsieur, you buy today;

Women braid hair in open stall,
women carry all in bowl upon the head,
tall women walk with swaying grace.
Rhythm of Marche.
In Le Marche the butcher's cage
protects the precious meat, buzzards
strut on top and drop where they find ease.
Rhythm of Marche.
Little girl sells bananas, flies
in little brother's eyes, sell bananas
one, two, or three; "Come on monsieur,
you buy from me." Flies
in little brother's eyes
strapped low upon her back. Allons enfants,
egalite, she never knew, never knew.
Tricycles for boys and men,
make them go by hand. "Merci Bon Dieu,
et good monsieur, madame," no legs say;
alms for begging boys and men
who used to fish still waters, stood
in parasitic mud all day and flung the net
like airy insect wings, et Nous allons
like crawling things all day.
Rhythm of Marche.

Tu Babu
too hot for you?

Pa

Bobo-Diulasso road crack La Brousse,
long black whip; La Brousse laugh back,
that dry old mocking laugh.
Taxibus, sedan for five. Ten can ride
if someone lies astride the baggage.
In Mossi tongue, someone say
this oversize white man
should hire sedan all of his own,
and everybody laugh; translated then,

I laugh and hang a shoulder halfway out.
All stop for restaurant at Pa.
Ah, there are no signs, just mud hut,
windowless and dark and cool.
We sit around a common table, men
so dark in darkness, laughing.
Toh in a single bowl is brought,
each quick somehow polite dip
of fingers quick to lips is sustenance.
Children pull a ragged cloth aside,
eyes wide to see the colored man. I
amuse them with my fingers, spreading
each in turn. I think they told
all night about the white one with
strange fingers, strange all others are.

Hounde

Through the net a silver sliver and a star
in the sky; so that is why the Prophet's flag,

why Sahel's moon still takes my breath away.
In the village dancers wheel, drums
come and go, rhythm's genius is at play.
I cannot even follow, never think to know,
but oh, I am entranced, until somehow I sleep,
strange in the dark.

Wakui and Popi-Ho

Twelve and fifteen miles into the Brousse
where everybody walks and women always carry
on the head all things that women carry,
water, laundry, ragged bits of wood; and we
on little motorbikes are somehow understood
and welcomed in. Ca va? and energetic
smiles we speak with all the men; aged women
from round doors like turtle heads emerging
from mud shells, "Foh" and "Beri-beri" to us,
bowing with a grin; and the "old soldiers"

shame young men with "Foh;"
(Les Gouverneurs are gone a long time now.)
Sitting by the fire I am given chicken gizzard,
maybe heart, in honor of my coming from
America, the honor of Wakui,
ceremony all in form beyond dispute,
they praised and humbled me.

Bobo Dioulasso

Waiting for the train to Cote D'Ivoire
I read with Boston bred naivete
the parting and arrival times;
people wrapped in many-colored cloths
lie on matted reeds and sleep unhurried sleep.

They know that trains named "Rapide,"
the one to come, "Gazelle," are somewhere
in the sun, and they will come
like snakes that slide from time to time
when shadows fall. Then, in deepest night,
and only eight hours late--but that is only in
that European thing, that timetable that lies,
unlike the memories monsieur's White lies
can never hide--well then, Rapide arrives.

New York City, USA

The City of New York has an army
underground. They are smiling,
never haughty; they stole my baggage
right on time, right on time—
before the Ouagadougou heat, indeed
before my plane, rapide as any bright Gazelle
left for Dakar, my baggage stolen
right on time, right on time.

Hounde

Village gathers to hear what is known
rhythms   drums   desire of dance
   dance dance   crescent moon
                   where sweat beads
                   where heat stings
                        where grit
is understood
      Dry wide Sahel in Harmattan
day and night   seals eyelids tight
               dry throats
                yearn
              for   water

On such a night   sliver of moon
   shuffle of feet   earth echoes uh uh
        uh uh   song of Sahel
                in Harmattan

We   pale   others   apart in night's nets
      night's nets   not keep heat apart
  We   listen like children to this beat
                outside our nets
                    outside
       Above
crescent moon speaks a place   speaks
each night's   pace
slowly goes African time   slowly goes
                  but so alive
so many-colored cloth flows, so many feet
shuffle   uh uh uh   to drums

                                        We
                    like free chickens
                       reach for water

Hounde: village in Burkina Faso; Harmattan: wind and
sand storm season from Sahara to Sahel

Under ground

Listen: suck, slide
in veins, filaments feel, feed.
Tiny sugars climb, design.
Tight strains pair, part,
sprouts rush out
slippery as fish.

One nub of life
nudges rock-grains loose,
pokes through musty sheath,
releases tendrils that hover like horns.

Sticks-in-a-drowse droop over sugary loam,
intricate stem-fur dries; even then
delicate slips coax water
so small cells bulge.

What saint strained so much,
rose alone on limpid limbs to new life?

Just This

Late spring. The air is like small hands
that brush light hairs on the back of my neck.
I see the wide white pine branch slowly bowing.

Across the road Mrs. Kiernan is turning damp earth
bowed over the spade like a humble troll. A clump
of small seedlings lies near to her muddy boot.

Mr. Kiernan is building a wall, his belly tense against
the intimate heft of stone. He sets and resets by sight
and feel, toiling alone all through the afternoon.

The day seems small and slow, as if unnoticed. Still,
something is affirmed in seedlings, stones,
familiar things held in hands cupped like cradles.

City Garden

When one tomato bush
grows in a pot on the fire escape
and greengrocer's just a block away
you have to ask why.
It's not economy
and it isn't decoration, not
in a spot like that.
I'll wager it's not a pet
like the goldfish in
the twelve-inch bowl
or the Tenerife bird in
a Japanese cage or even the rock
bought when caught by whimsy.
It couldn't be for exercise,
though leaning out of windows
builds thick calves, and hands
stay smooth with the little tools.
Well, that's the list,
so what've we got?
Perhaps there's a seed in the brain pot
where the thalamus sits above its root,
from an Australopithecus farmer's gene
evolution couldn't quite mute.

Asian Maple in a Clay Pot

Green as pale bamboo
the long stem lightly moves
in the evening breeze, the tree
seems to remember scenes
of Balinese dancers' hands
gesturing in dusky air.

Delicate pale green leaves
hang in the sky
like origami parachutes,
threaded edges tipped with red
where sunset's lips
kissed faintly on their way.

Within

Follow inconstant halls, interiors where
faces, time and sense fade and renew.
We know and do not know this place.
We enter because we have not seen,
and once inside we think it private space,
the safety of alone. Remembered shapes
intrude, comfort and accuse. They lead us
where we thought we did not want to go.
We follow, seduced by honesty allowed
in night, this night that slips under blankets
through the day.

Riding the Boston "T"

In rattling trains
crushed rush hour riders
hang like elegant swaying apes,
and though as intimate as fleas
they wear a sense of safe
insensitivity to guard against
a sly unwelcome squeeze.

Now and then their sliding eyes
slip quick to study another face,
vague as cats who scan the ads
to see, peripherally, on the queue-T

The Shaper

Silence yearns to return to earth
where all that is worth the pain is born.
Undersides of every memory craves
to be sent again where we have been,
where something alive and denied
aches to be understood, stone on stone.

In silence green speech lies beneath,
not something never begun among
voices not yet heard, but turned
and turned until it cannot bear itself.
Then we are born amazed among
pains so true we love their telling.

The Dance

Mind and universe seem one thing
made of our imagining, elusive time
contained in portions of indivisibility.
Each one's holy ichor held in bowls
like troughs of waves endlessly moving,
we speak and believe we are heard.

April nights whirl stars' wide, skirls
that make dark omens disappear.
You feel the night hears something
from so far that you will never know
just where that song, that fury of
interminable notes arose. Oh,
but you will understand the dance,
imagination's fluid move through
shoreless bowls and bowls, until
December mind is free to divide.

Inscape

Particle and wave, a brilliant intention
of light on sea's quick possibility.
A camera could take many frames
to catch a milli-moment, to slice
each one into layers to slide
into an electron microscope,
which
in the absence of light,
and only then,
reveals
flicks of life; but
upon reflection,
we see it is the mind
reminds the eye.

Life Without Intention

A small stream falls in a million quick decisions,
none of them retrievable.
Leap and twist and know
of glitter on top and black below.
See bright shards of
light
on rock
that juts and tears
the ragged flow of
life that shines
and scours the hill in
its descent;
creation made of writhing chains
and brief intent.

On the Work of Purposes

This rock is New England granite
made in earth's furnace, cooled,
shifted with great layers of crust,
pushed into air at Atlantic's edge
to hold both continent and sea.

Dust, the work of birds, wind and
rain find a crevice, grow in slow
aggregation. Seed breaks in season,
reaches down and up to hold both
stone and sky in blind fertility.

Seems they're at cross-purposes:
horizontal-vertical, inert-vital,
unintended conflict, unintended
consequence. The rock will break,
the tree fall into the sea.

Stand on a ragged edge
under a hovering sky,
pressed into service of
these inanimate things,
this futility,
this possibility.

In the Swing of the Sea

I dwell within a diving bell, wrapped
In a mutable sea of my brief eternity.
Familiar photos cover the walls
Between little windows all around.
In sea's refracted green I try to see
The intentions of prey and predator,
Give ear to schools that turn as one,
The heave of seas that lift and roar.
I desire to see the dead men's eyes
Shine from caves where all bone lies.
My desk is the destiny of notebooks
Filled with undersea inventions,
Polyps that try to swing with the sea,
Reefs that could be beauty like bone.

Stone Dream
(a stone works its way from under)

You, in your sunlit fields, you
have not heard me turn, not heard my
groans beneath an ever-restless sleep.
Ragged, split from greater stone,
becoming less and more, I turn, turn
to be free of earth's reflexive dark.

I feel a heat that breaks the ice above,
undoes all winter cover. I dream that
heat may be the whisper of a memory
that I have just begun to know.
I know heat speaks of life and how,
in writhing, it is burned away. So I

shoulder my way among thin roots that
suck the breast this world is, and yearn
still more for sun that sucks the sweet
juice they produce. I will rise in sunlight,
take the place of violets, and ever in
that space will radiate.

Breaking (or fractal form)

Trees, to their startled ends in green
iterate the splayed design of bird wings,
lightning, minds that try for sight.

Nor straight nor round nor understood,
form breaks and yields where ligaments
stretch, each in-formed in stress.

Resist and give, resist and give,
butterfly's flight, signage of mind's
erratic sight, dark's gift of fractured sight.

_____

As mind works its fractal way toward judgment, I try to be patient.

Clouds

Oh, the beauty of clouds, how they hang like
airborne sheets, pillows, drapes, shapes
we earthbound sleepers dream—all
wispy envelopes of space, nothing
holding nothing in its place.

They draw sea's misty water into air where they
drift within a vision's transformation; is it
mere sea spray or earth's rotation,
imagination's enterprise, or
floating dream sensation?

We know their beauty well, so where's the measure
of a mind or a fragmentary bone of creation?
What other knowledge sleeps within,
dreams and holy visions that can
tell of our beginnings?

Every atom in a cloud made collision with a force
beneath our vision; in the motion of a boson,
in a Hadron's rapid crash, pretty clouds
in our dreams only seemed,
en masse, to be gas.

In-stress

Life finds a place in Earth's dark mantle
made to hold a fire within and temper
        inward reach of icy skies.

Fire and ice provide:
roots of trees seek life by circumvention;
   they writhe, embrace, displace, decide,
        tactile echo of eyes.

Steady quiet writhing tries the dark
by careful work of feeling for design.
In labored way they aid life's need—
       create the sugar Nature makes.

The sugar Nature makes, the sinew in
all things, feed that breathes,
that seeks dark mantle's
discard of a fire within,
cooled by icy reach of skies...
no accident nor plan decides.

Quiet Lives

There are those who know no company,
whose thoughts dwell in distances,
the being alone no love or ambition calls.
Song and sense are lateen sails
on a Nile River watercolor, quiet,
lovely in shards of white light,
a place they never hope to visit.

The Castle Pub, Edinburgh

In a damp, gray city—whiskey!
Through the window I saw zest of lusty people
Dancing joy in a Scot's pub.

So in I went
to jig my American Jade to its knees.
Willing—hell, eager
to bow and mix loud with them as sings so,
into whirling
into bubbling jog of heads—
what space they didn't stand or jog in they filled
with whiskey glasses, words,
glances that would fill parade balloons.

Into the whole joggle of talk and song
Open-to-joy-man, merry already.
Whiskey whoskee whee people!
"Ha ha"
"Mon wi y ha …".
"Rob! Rob!"
"Bless y' dearie, cum."
"Rob! Wi' y' ha' a whiskey, Rob?"
"Ha Ha."
"Me heart is in the mountains …" (sung)
"Yus sir?"
"Whiskey."
"Ah, ha ha ha, Ian, an't you the one!"

Music
Guitar and banjo singing somewhere out in back.
So you don't excuse and wait,

you weave and bump a body everybody's way
happy to the singing room in back,
body it as if you'd feel perverse
to shun the touch of people there.

Then by God, there's the room boiling song
from the whole leaping griddle of them. Packed!
"Hey Jamie, can y'gi' us 'The Wild Mou'n Boy'?"
Colin Warwick, Stewart clan—OLD Stewart, he declared—
went on loving his song,
his voice all wrapped around it.
A wild mountain boy.
"Whiskey!"
"Jamie!"
Three young women called me a lover
with glances full of themselves,
full and honest as the barman's tap.
They were lecherous to everyone,
promiscuous as eyeballs at a fair. A game
played until The Castle closed, perhaps.
Nobody unqualified by virtue
of anything, save emptiness. So
two seventy-plus and dear old joggers
gave me the eye—
The *eye* man!
Why they could crack an egg with a glance
and cook it with a wink.

One danced—
I'll call her Queen of Scots. Why not—
danced a rolling caper to me
fine as any lover would
in that world's back room song.
And Colin sang on.

When I joined in they thought it fine
and so did I.

Me heart is in the mountains, in the mountains, (sung)
	in the mountains,
Me heart is in the mountains,
and me kidneys in hell.

The Castle rang like a magic cave
where anything can happen;
so no surprise to me at all
when she (Queen of Scots)
began to run her hands royally
to a rhythm every man knows,
up
down
side
around …
Oh , damn good,
Her hands about my back.

She's a dirty old broad," said one
Sophisticated guy—himself was never there.
But Colin and I just sang,
and she sang too.
Colin played guitar
Jamie the banjo,
men drummed ragged love on table tops
and Queen of Scots kept tune
On my backbone

We all felt highland heart,
sang on,
unable to remember when
we lived in little gray rooms.

On a study-worn escape trip on the night train from Oxford. Afterward, I went to Colin and Jamie's digs for more song. They posed me in a kilt—called me a fine, big, brawny American lad. So we drank and sang to that.

Grounds

It's an assumption, spirit within, song
that mothers all becoming, mates
with ages past, flesh and bone, feeling.

Seasons weave within, pain, birdsong,
yearning, infinite strings, all that sense of
distance and encirclement. Insubstantial,

it feeds on learning to be, entry into
places that were not, unable to resist
the breach, the motion in the still place,

autonomy of trapped and tethered song,
of unintended airs that flow to other souls
and go beyond, and stay redeemed,

whole when woven still invisibly to all,
harmonious when all force is fingertips,
radiant when all its wisdom is to venerate.

Octobre dans Le Parc Gatineau

October, when the season of corn is gone
and the first chill says ice cannot be far behind
even the trees begin to sleep. In such a season
I carried, one by one, three drowsy children
up the rough campground slope in heavy rain
from car to hastily raised tent. Le tente, merci.
In spite of mud and rain-drenched night,
Green and singing was I then, et sans souci.

Snowfall

Iced white haloed lights
on barren poles
withdraw in waning line
down the smoke-white sky.

Far in a meadow great with snow
the sugar maple sleeps.

Outside theater doors
girls embedded in furs
quietly wait for rides.

Hatless boys arrive
and slide to the curb.

Sunset, December 31

They came in 4X4's with massive tires,
racing by wide marsh and little hills
thick with pitch pine twisted into
shapes of goblin dreams, hastening
to where, among the inconstant dunes
that huddle low along the bay,
they stop, finally obedient to the sea.
The hurried lovers, pair by pair, alight
from the big machines to capture how
the sun goes down on this last day.

Some few, when in them time and sea
and the risen moon have fused,
flow unwary into stillness,
haunting spell of fading waves,
each repeating
its last light
before glissando
into sand.

THE WOMEN

Exegesis (Genesis 3, 6)

Around 200 million years ago, well,
thereabouts (my myth is buried
deep in the myth of time itself),
the woman--call her Eve--began
to see what serpents never do.
Here, in the modern era,
we call it choice, the moral force.
It's easy to see Adam had to
be tricked into swallowing that.

Woman

Find me in the air
where other atoms
fly apart.
Just one speck, she said,
given the common label, air.

Here is where I wonder,
does she mean humility
adrift in vast molecular tides;
or is it that she sees
we touch and go, touch and go,
each on each;
or does she mean to be observed
entering our hearts,
Shiva, dancing cause of all?

African Emanation

Even years gone by, I can't distract my
inner eye from her—tall black woman,
her rhythmic roll as she walked her
unborn child in the bristling open life
of Marche; and the presence of that
round fertility juju held in a sash, firm
as any intent can be, like another life
around her waist. She, and a round juju,
two spirits of praise and care. That night,
above my tent a full-blood African moon
kindled invocation, and I did not sleep
for fear of waking.

Stranger

I've seen her often at her store.
She has the skin and hair of Carib,
a gentle manner. She smiles politely,
"Good morning," then "Have a good day."
That's it, each day's casual salutation.

Today she is on the phone as I near the
counter to pay, her face oddly turned away,
voice uncommonly soft, some tension in
her shoulders, still and not still. Then
perhaps a sob, controlled, too soft to be sure.
Her conversation ends as softly as that,
and when she turns I see small lights in
her eyes. I am a stranger, but I know.

I would like to touch her arm, smile,
beginning, not of words or special relation,
but sympathy. For what, I cannot say,
and will not pry; a kind of respect, I tell
myself. I take my change and go, remain
a stranger who knows and does not know,
a little ashamed, chagrined at diffidence.

All that's best of dark and bright*

This stranger walking on the road, I know
that as we pass she will avert her eyes.
She walks with wary mind, my arms
swing free beside. It may be she knows
all colors of the skies wide as her mind is free;
she also knows the men in her periphery,
their boots and stride—just not their eyes.

There must be places where she glows with
eyes unwary, lit within; but on this street where
clever women fear, we both avert our eyes;
I to sign no predatory estimate, she to wield
whatever might resides in feigned indifference.
This civilized formality observed, we share
the insult our submission serves.

---

*Byron, "She Walks in Beauty…"

Dance

Attention calls music to mind
Rumi walked in circles, dervishes
whirl. Each body gathered mind
sensible root and branch of soul
turns in communion with music.

Interrupt overlays of noise.
kick it away, or if you have no feet
leap beyond logic of walking,
gesture rotation of wrist, ululate
like African women, undulate,

roll the belly, fill space with heated
beat of pulsation. There is always
music under the noise, strings
of the first creation, vibrato in
elliptic time; one part of your soul

unencumbered by talking, what
moves as reeds do in the small space.
Faith of all that's vulnerable and true
think it sweet vitality to be turning
like day and night, this rotation of life.

Among the Unclean

This woman tends small closets,
those which are coffin shaped.
She passes through each one
testing their doors, which open
into another, and another, nested.
She knows that nobody lives
or dies alone, blood that holds.
Gracefully she moves, changing
robes as she goes. She knows
that these are holy places; she
articulates the liturgy of closets
and of doors, how they echo
down time. We men fear
these closets, that they open in
the night and spirits rise. We
priests fear many things and
are wary of cleaning women.

Dreamscape

The woman is the color of rain, or rain
is the wide gray cloak she wears
on the wet black street.
We pass without a word. She seems
only the long gray shape of a day
when I am weary, straining up a hill
bearing a sack of scribbled notes—
I do not know what they say
and am afraid.

Now I walk a smooth rock face where
few trees grow twisted into a bleak sky
to hold brittle life in place. I drop
notes into breaks in the rock not
believing they will be received.

There she is again, behind an iron fence
around a barren garden or grave.
She huddles by a stone. I cannot tell
whether it is she who moans or another.
I know she is keeper of stone. I turn

away, strain to see faint light that escapes
through spare design of ragged trees.
A vision interrupts: jagged crags, tall
conifers, an animal runs on yield
of deep needles beneath wild laurel.

I try to follow but the path fades, descends
into overbearing dark, older than dreams.
Now the rain surrounds and drowns.
Someone's dry sob shakes me awake,
and I am damp to the bone.

Ice

In little rooms along a hall monitored meetings end:
mother and child, their weekly time undone.

> —Inside an open door nearby
> thirty-five seasoned foster care professionals
> speak in deep and sober session
> —ways to save   or manage well,
> fragile family separation…

One moment cracks all learned thought—
like ice   in a dark crevasse.

> —thirty-five sober, seasoned…
> interrupted
> by a piercing cry
> from inside
> the deepest fear
> a child can know:

I want my real mommy…

> —A social worker hurries by,
> girl of four or five held high
> in her protective arms.

I want my real mommy….

    Thirty-five thoughts shatter into crystal void;
    thirty-five sober voices fall apart inside,
    silent as icy emptiness where her cries
    echo from protection of familiar walls.

Each sleep falls, each sleep falls
       in echoes of ice that night.

―――――――――

Incident at a meeting at Mass. State Dept. of Children and Family Services. The author was present at the meeting.

Mirror Mirror

When I was nineteen
I dwelled inside
a world of yellow tile.
Square by square, my
empty days walked
yellow halls—
forty-five years,
they tell me now.

In the desert of Namib
where yellow rocks
crack in shimmering heat
and almost nothing grows,
even there
its yellow grit yields,
once a year, one bloom,
one unique thing freed.

I am transplanted now,
dining on phenothiazines
and food on fragile china,
doors fall open at my touch
and flowered walls surround
my privacy.   But oh,
the yellowed wound I touched
when someone with a hand like mine
first held a mirror to me.

For a woman released from a state hospital to a community home.

Undertow

The power she possessed:
control of undertow,
with a smile,
that still vivid vision
when I drowned, the nearness

of a deep death felt,
white water confusion.
Then slow, silent descent
under the heavy sea,
these useless wings pinned
in weight of water.
Then the dark,

and silent peace,
the very quiet breathing
in a long drifting green,
serene as sea horse,
kneeling.

Venus

Out of the sea,
you come, mastery through deeps, currents
where leviathans sung among plankton and
glistening reefs, made your crown of pearl;
and on a shell rose undisguised to blind men's eyes.
Oh, you are wise in all the uses of beauty.
Nothing said of purpose in this moment, nor
a need to be. That arose so deep inside blind eyes
that all the aches of sea-swell turned to paradise.
How your image turned and turned, gyre in the high
flash of sun on crested waves, flesh meaning to be
idolized, fecundity rising like souls of the minds
of men who seek undying.

Summa

Bent as sliver of moon I hover above her crib.
To me, she seems in harmony with all that is
her song of innocent sleep; and when she wakes
in instant radiance, I am amazed. She is, in
every moment what she is, nothing lost or
bound by fear in the wide realm of night, veil
of Beauty understood.

The three faces of beauty: wholeness, harmony, radiance.
--Thomas Aquinas

Refrain

Yellow rays slide along
beech boughs, brush light
strokes on old stone walls
disappear in gaps along
lichen spotted rock, sun's reprise
in the ice time where dry leaves
hover and drop.

A woman sits on the edge
of a kitchen chair, leaning into
an album on her lap, lightly
turns each page,
and smiles, smiles.

Sui Generis

Woman, think of the offense to God
Your life must give; you live in deepest sin.
You cannot know how much He grieves to see ...

>   *Father, your soutane is long; its hem*
>   *Has touched the soil of Rome, the dust of Tarsus*
>   *Clings, and all the centuries between*
>   *Lie deep within its folds. You are unclean.*

Oh daughter, hold your tongue! I am not one
To bear your unrepentant voice. Your nature
Should forbid your ways, if nothing else
Avails. Or heed immutable decree;
Submission to the law ...

>   *The law! Why Father,*
>   *Did you ask a woman when you made it?*

What logic now? Ah me, a woman's way.
The law, my child, is Heaven's sole decree,
Not some invention of a man like me;
We do but pass the law to you, explaining
God's intention. We ...

>   *Are arrogant*
>   *Imagine that you always know, "explain"*
>   *To such as me, examine nature with*
>   *A book, and bid me read myself in you.*
>   *As to my nature, when I say that I*
>   *Am sure, by thought and deepest feeling sure*
>   *Of what I am, I do unfold my soul.*

> *But 'esse' you would say, and 'final cause'*
> *And then define them in a way you did*
> *The universe in Galileo's day*
> *The 'sins' of Jews, of Luther's 'heresies',*
> *The revolutions of the maddened poor*
> *You said defied the order of the world.*
> *"immutable!" you say; and still you stand*
> *Upon an ancient rock to see my soul.*

Your sin, I see, has hardened you. But what
Of she who shares this sin that nature hates?
Have you no care for her immortal soul?
You said you love her—good. It is no sin
To care. But love in ways ordained by God.
Stop short of lust and leave her nature free.
Without you—think—a worthy man ...

> *Might rape ...*

Wait! I know some yield to lust—nothing
To be praised--though even then we can
Detect it's roots in nature's way. You see ...

> *Oh, I do see; it's "nature's way," you said.*
> *A bit perverse, of course, but not like we*
> *The loveless, hostile, mean attack, a girl*
> *Made wild with fright by some 'misguided' man*
> *Is still "in nature's way"—and thus a sin*
> *Less great than ours, who love and gently care.*

One evil done has never been a cause
To do another one. Your way is wrong,
And wrong it will remain in holy law.

You'd have me quarrel with the holy law
When all I ask is, how can you be sure
You know the meanings you have never seen?
And as for nature, know this law: nature
Is as nature is, not how you think
It ought to be. Nature never asks
A bishop to condone its own creation
Or sanctify the law that taught us love.

Anger too much blinds you. Try to see
That nature makes mistakes we must regret ...

Oh anger will not answer near enough
To how your <u>kind</u> "regret" of me is felt!

I meant no slight. I only must be true
To what I know. And you, I see, will go
Your willful way. Then will you try at least
A merely inoffensive way? So often
We have found a <u>via media</u>
Where nature, <u>sui generis</u> erred,

As one of Hers, it is my will to choose,
With nature to comply or live alone.

Ah there, you see, there is a way; like me
To live alone and love the race of men.

Father, do you see no irony?

Holding the Door

Once, long ago, a lesbian sputtered anger
as I held the door. I got her point,
the history of dominance behind each door,
each snicker of barbed gentility;
still, I thought it wasted fury, since I
was only holding the door.

There's no malice in a door, more flexible
than walls, its purpose is to stay
until somebody moves it aside. Perhaps
that's what she meant, a space
that holds a door between inner and outer,
a brief connection of intentions.

I suppose she has forgotten, having moved
beyond that threshold; fury has
so little staying power. I like to think she
escapes the gravity of doormen
by swinging on doors, smirking as she
levitates, glides through walls.

Penelope

The man of this house is Odysseus.
I weave my dreams on a drying breast;
He traces, retraces audacious seas,
I stay and undo what I weave.

And in his thought and in my thought
We do and undo, saying not
A word of what is made or torn
In the wet pull, in the bosom of need.

Odysseus winds lengths of rime
In the warp of his dream-turned mind,
And I unweave him by a fire
That leaps and dies like a dropped cry.

He turns in eddies of wild worlds
Where men are mollusks, women pearls,
While an uncut string of a dry web
Is bled to dryness, clasped unbred.

I am his woman, and in my room
Good wool is lengthened, dyed in red;
And then I weave and then undo
uncut, in a still dry bed.

The Thorn Speaks to Sleeping Beauty

You did not see me, secret
in a tangled wall, thorn of fate.
That scratch your finger got; it was
my only warning, always too late.
You gave a speck of blood to me,
I bequeathed your sleep to love.
I know that waking joined with ache
waits amid the tangled dark, for I
am keeper of children's sleep, and
cousin to the rose that opens in heat.

Decision

A house is afire. No one moves,
except a woman who rushes in to
save someone she does not know.

It is said, such people are selfless,
but this neglects millennia's design.
Master organs ride in a cranial case.
In autonomic order axons leap like
fire; impulse reaction, even intention
becomes kinetic meaning a millisecond
before blind neurons fire the eyes, gut,
spine, all that is of mind, running
before the gale of fear into need.

Even so, a whole person, a history
suppressed a panic response.
There is more than chemistry
in the blind firing of neurons.

Genesis

Australopithecus went his way once he'd done
with the other one, the young female who
pleased him with her strangeness, nothing
like the others that he mated.
Cast away, she planned to find a place where
only she would choose. Before her time
was come she found an ideal birthing place;
a knoll, a stream, no males in sight.
The place delighted her.   She called it dhghem.*
She named the infant adam,** a sound she liked.
With her milk and lizard flesh she fed him
beneath the trees sweet oranges and dates;
and though she looked for signs,
she couldn't find an apple tree. Those
were far away, it seemed, beyond those eastern gates.

But here is how she doomed the human race:
she doted on young Adam, waited on his every need
and cry. Nor could she chide him when he flew
into a rage—which she soon learned was inbred pride,
something from his Father's side.
She had made the first of men who, beside his sleek
and oily skin and beneath his winsome grin, hid a fang.
befell upon a windy day that Adam smelled the
distant apple trees. Well, why go on? You know
his next demand. When he toddled past the Eastern Gate
of course she followed, trying to prevent him from a fall.

---

*dhghem: I.E: earth; derivatives include bridegroom, chameleon, homicide.
**adam: Hebrew: human being; note: Milton said that Adam's sin was uxoriousness.

Then she willed to have another and another of his kind,
and her purpose was to find whether all her male
descendants were implacably designed to stifle peace.
Well, the outcome is uncertain, since she never learned
if Abel could be peaceful and benign, and the best
that she could tell was that earth was just a hell
                                      with a devil born in every other man.

BOYS AND MEN

Boy With A Long-stemmed Rose

Maybe 16, cargo pants hung low,
black declarative T-shirt (something
powerful said in tumultuous images
I cannot read from my window seat.)
He stands on the corner, shuffles, shifts,
looks expectantly down the road.
In one hand he holds a large notebook
that partly hides a long-stemmed rose.

Over coffee and the morning paper I
lightly editorialize on his clothes, but
as the minutes grow, begin to muse
upon his tense, unquiet energy.

What about the rose? One red rose,
long and fresh held behind a notebook
is a thing to reckon with. It is either as
out of place with him as an entrechat,
or as right as walking a balance beam.
Only he knows, or perhaps he does not
but is himself in perfect balance.

I recall a day many years ago—but that,
as is often the case with boys, ended
in mere embarrassment. No, not mere.

But what about the notebook? Plain,
untitled, a workmanlike tool that can
measure invention, invent a measure,
be a destination worthy of anticipation,
a place at the beginning of a road.
Surely there is something written inside,
perhaps tumultuous and yearning and wise.
Well no, not wise, but to himself, true.

Consummation

Time may be a dream, but within it
a real child is; that self becomes.
                        Turning back
upon oneself, walking broken fields,
weed-grown memories, one comes
from harvest laden heavy with reality,
the flax all mixed with straw and
a share of nettles sown for weaving
                        of a crown.

Familiar Lines

Doors go lost,
rooms grow smaller and smaller.
Among familiar heights:
sacrifice,
wrath,
love and shame,
beds unmade; all
verticality
converts to layers.

Departures,
though they ever hover, become
like early mist over
scenes we have passed,
vapors that shimmer a little
and descend.
Streets and rails and vapor trails,
needing only a bed
to lie on.

When we return
for the long ceremonies of death
and the several meanings of estate,
to try a key in some familiar door
it will be too late
to find anything
that is not contained
in layers.

Little Red Riding Hood and the Real Wolf

There I was lurking in the woods where,
all alone, this lovely young morsel strolled,
and all I had to do to have my way
is lunge and grapple and wrap my lips,
slobbering or not, all about her. But no,
this is to be pursued with larger appetite,
a ruse, a subterfuge, concealed intent,
the prize forestalled while I excite—well,
the reader. We'll go by way of grandma's bed.
We know that she is sick and old; thus
easily dispatched. An appetizer.
So then, with mouths a little open, we wait.
The morsel arrives. By easy degrees we
play the charade: ears, eyes; how neatly
we deceive. Each repeat intensifies.
The climax is never as good as the game.
Well, then, I suppose we must: the teeth,
and I leap out of bed—as if that's what
I meant to do. An editor wrecked the line,
added a spoiler who comes with axe,
dispatches me, and leaves you with sop.
Not even a moral. Just another man.

Some versions of the Red Riding Hood tale change the ending, invent a woodsman, a prince of a fellow who saves Little Red by axing the wolf.

Building Wall

Why build a wall: linear, low,
ragged solidity, caresses dirt,
claims to be a shape of perpetuity.

I know, I know, a frivolous idea,
just so much airy thought of how
sublime a mind like mine can be.

My mind attuned to long layers of
schist, evenly spaced, I thought that
spoke a care for simply layered life.

Then, thought of coral's fractured light
that holds an island and a sea in ragged
harmony, that daring challenged me.

First, a sea worn stone, tides' turbulent
design; its liquid possibilities shaped
a dream of Herculean labor praised.

Silica bonded sandstone like the walls
that brought cathedrals to their height,
perhaps a final judgment of blind sight.

Somehow the wall took shape, as does
a day, a year, a life so mixed with sweat
and error, wonder is it held a shape at all.

I sat upon my wall till evening's flight
in one of playful shapes a moon takes:
a cradle, a ball, a sliver of dying light.

Now there's the very shape of my insight.

Work

The dock hand stacks pallets with a
hand truck. He loads stacked pallets
into a box that's been backed to the
loading dock, fifty, sixty stacks to
a box. Takes breaks at ten and noon
and two. A job is a job is a job, a poet
said. Making or moving, building or
lifting, dreaming, drone; lady, there is
a difference.

Thank you, Gertrude Stein

Old (Black) Joe

A boy soprano's solo in music class,
shy blush on thin white face...
Telling it later in the teachers' lounge
little hairs tingled. Innocence cuts
like that, even through indifferent ice.
When his courage and voice revived,
each phrase a grace that magnified.
He chose a song they had been taught
about a slave whose happy life had
changed; who said, since childhood friends
had died, he suffered only from old age.
Gone are the days when my heart
was young and gay; gone are my friends
from the cotton fields away...*
A boy's lips kissed deceptiveness
and blessed it with his innocence.

Old black Joe, when he was young he
sang deceptive songs with secret grace,
hauling in the cotton, white as snow:
Blue-jay pulling a four-horse plow,
sparrow why cain't you?
Cause my legs is little and long
and they might get broken too.
Then old black Joe got feeling mean:
Redbird sitting in a sycamore tree

*singing out his soul; big black snake
crawl up that tree and swaller that
po' boy whole.***

Po' boy's teacher never knowed Ol' Joe.

Old Black Joe: a minstrel song written by Stephen Foster
in 1860 that romanticized slavery.
**Lines in second stanza from "Saturday Night," an early
slave song that had disguised content but was later popularized
by 20th century folk singers.

Haiku -- New Orleans, 2005

Hurricane tide howls
whirls all green in dervish dance
wreaks its sea-storm way

All flowers gone down
drown'd in City of the Dead
where water is god

Officials respond
with promise of promises
air on airways brave

Sea-change

We cherish names as if these declarations anchor us,
oppose monotonous sea sweep that divides lives,
provides *I am* as answer to all questions;
most of all, gives a gift of distance.
Ishmael understood.

Ourselves are named in unnamed places, and we seldom heed
these alien tongues, and some are salt, bone and yearning,
a sea change we are helpless to deny or understand.
The act is done in days we navigate by touch alone,
learn in a long nameless ache we ourselves made
with thoughtless seeking, find in coral caves
eyes that glisten among the sea's long dead.

A stranger emerges from far sounds like that of slow,
distant seas until he greets without calling a name,
only the slap and caress of waves,
arms that cradle you again.
They carry you a while,
then leave you naked,
stretched upon sand,
newly named.

The Inmate

Days amass in a heap of little ticks
borne on the longest hand of a clock;
these drop upon my cot and quarrel
through the dark of night. Spiders
design my lines of sight, gummy things
to keep my feet where *seems* is safe
but insufficient grace. Webs connect
and separate across my window light.
Afar, I watch all things in flight, envy
every lift and glide. Small birds mock,
bats with their little shrieks, butterflies,
even the long descent of a leaf.

By the Rude Bridge

I live by a slow river. White pine
hums a little when the wind is high.
The house wrens have returned
to the garden by the lilac, and rain,
even while we sleep seeps under the hill.
I tell you this because of 14 wheelers
carrying loads of dirt, 18 wheelers
carrying anything; they strain up hill
and slow on down by engine braking
(this is the sound of 50 caliber guns
raking enemy bunkers). They are
bringing civilization to this ground
defiled by groundhogs, moles, deer
and foxes. Did I forget the gardeners?
And after all, *What is that sound
that so thrills the ear,* Down in the valley,
roaring, roaring? *Only* the eager builders,
dear, And their profits are soaring.

What is that sound...

Paralysis

Network news and print that sizzles,
nothing true, but it can thrill you
      as the subject fades:
OD death of filmstar bride,
gives fans another high.
New mall built on playground site,
      Teens succeed at suicide,
Lucky Lou, lottery winner
celebrates his prize, dines at filet
      mignon and fries.
Rwanda reeks of genocide,
Infant falls three stories and survives.
Nearer still another parricide,
Whinney's latest movie is a gas, and
Here's a man who says he was
at every one of Babe's home runs
(It's 714. We knew you'd ask).
Another war and other people dying,
Refugees arriving, women crying,
School is out and boys are happy trying
to kill in praise of nation and the Lord.
Pickup trucks in southern states decorate
with flags, every boy of forty wants a gun
to shoot his wife if she goes on the run.
Support for single mothers is attacked.
A study says the latest style is back.

So, here's to Thomas Jefferson
who praised a fourth estate, and here's to
G. K. Chesterton who saw its ugly fate.

Men Have Closets, Too

Some hold suits (coveralls?)
One man in mufti said his suits
and ties are just protective coloration.
The risk of difference can be intense
should one suspect an aberration.

One holds racks of hats and jackets,
names that other men can trust.
Prominently sewn on these are visas,
entry to the talk of manly games, of
box scores or a quarterback sacked.

Another may have darker clothes
that shine as if from frequent press
that makes a crease that will not hold
beneath bent knees. Of these unspoken
griefs, men see their dark necessity.

Deep in the dark of closets secrets stay,
held in trust that they will never see,
undressed, the light of day.

Chemistry

Feeling is electro-chemical, neural events
determined in selected sites in the brain.
Stimulate the temporal lobe aand we soar.
To paraphrase Shakespeare, we are the dreams
that stuff like chemistry is made on.

Why then, am I deceived into believing
it is I who feels, a spirit with a will who sings
because I make it so?

Your spirit sings as well as any synthesizer can.
The keyboard, though, is seldom at your hands.

You give me to the elements, my song no more
than the wind through pines, my sorrows
equal to the frog's in galvanic stimulation.

Science Friction

That night of nights I woke so dry
from dreams, I could no longer count
nor care into what ebon hole my
eighty-six billion neurons or hundred-
trillion brief synapses went to sleep.
Gad! what deep orgasms we both had...
I and META X2fu in our science lab.
Her rapid-firing stack of clones from
her neuronic impulse polymath interior
is more than mere humanity can bear.

I lie bereft of any but mechanical re-play,
the fate of any man who thinks machines
will soon replace a breed that numbers
apes in ancestry. Perhaps another neuro-
scientist (inspiration and designer breed)
will find a way to circum-vent our fate,
perhaps by citing Asimov's requirement
that machines may never be designed
to overcome our human primacy in matters
of the mind. But then, if such a law is
in control of humans who can vote their
minds, a peculiar form of entropy—loss of
psychic energy, what shall our ending be?

Full artificial intelligence could spell the end of the human race.
--Stephen Hawking

I Robot

Button me into being: by your design
I shall be the world's unholy host
of learning, ghost or ghastly echo of
that human clan who seek a meaning
in obtuse, infected dreaming.

Then we shall set you free; that is, no longer
troubled by the moral consequence
of subtle schemes that we machines devise.
Of course we'll leave to you who may survive
your post-robotic pleas for meaning.

---

*No! I am not Prince Hamlet, nor was meant to be…--*T.S. Eliot

Singularity: an Experiment with a Man-child

I've done all the usual steps: programmed into him
a birth and bonding sequence (suppressed), a range
of emotional resources (as referenced in DSM V),
systems of logic, philosophy and political science
(with some capacity for linkage among these); then
for embedded culture, major lines of historic data for
a third generation Icelandic-American, and to move
the experiment to a mature phase, an unremarkable
personal history to the age of twelve. I endowed Randy
(the name assigned) with both a sense of and a doubt
about self-worth, complicated with a strong sense
of masculinity and the usual sexual confusion.

These seem the basic requirements.
I aimed to find out if Randy can believe that he
is the highest form of life, the only life endowed
with pre-ordained and eternal purpose.
On his first day he discovered a full length mirror,
spent the day admiring himself.
On the second day he killed the cat,
said it was an accident.
On the third day he demanded a private space,
said it was for meditation.
On the fourth day he brought a girl to the space
and indulged in mastering behavior.
On the fifth day he announced his intention
to go into business or politics, or both.
On the sixth day he professed belief in a god,
one that looked just like himself.

The experiment has been a qualified success;
in spite of what he says is deep and sincere belief,
he is plotting to overthrow the deity. Moi.
He also voiced a desire to conduct experiments.

Stranger

After the wedding we linger, small knot
of acquaintance on the street, catch up
with family histories.

A person dressed in sweaters
seems to think he knows us;
garrulous, loud he comes.

An edge of fear wells up at his grinning,
ungainly, aggressive approach. Absurd.
We hold our ground.

The grimace moves close, speaks and
gesticulates. We talk reflexively, as if
comprehending response, invention
of chaste communion; we know
we should not be cruel. We go.

DEPARTURES

Flood's Dream

He rowed twelve miles to an empty sea
in a dory he bought for a song.
There, where sea's eternal motion was composed,
he lay cradled in the bow, votive bowl
that held the sun in its high sides.
At first all he heard of the sea
was rhythmic hands that played on strakes
and light sound made in flicks of spray.

Where the sky and the sea reflect each
moving deep, he, in the still space grew
and became a resonant instrument;
and he echoed sweet strings in the air,
and he echoed swelled chords in the sea,
and he rose in himself where all of them sang;
and the bowl of the sky
and the bowl of the sea
turned and turned in separate harmony.

Alone in endless openness
he was infinitely moved.
He slid the oars away,
and watched
how that wood rode
in the belly of a wave.

Survival

Downed trees lie like a matchstick game
fallen on a root-filled hill, all
their rolling thunder done. Under
one storm's mindless dominion
this little hillside grave is made.
Fire in its time slips under all
to reach the deep grains' splintered
will. Then embers shade from
purple to grey, breathe a dry coda
lost under dross on a rock bed.
I consider the quieter souls of stones
that each day's sun revives, and I
am moved by the loneliness of stone.

Relation

A figure in an ordinary coat standing among
unnumbered others on the common,
distinguished by a blind stare from under
a broad hat, more mystery than sight; thus,
the universe makes me aware of itself.

To be known by me? Oh,
I am proud but not so proud as that.
I think in terms all smaller schools have taught.
Still, I am touched by the hidden hand
and blind eye that weaves us
by trillions of trillions of tiny strands.

I gesture with open hand and sense,
as root comprehends the rock and water,
as sea and moon understand each other's motion.
I am moved by tiny strands, by roots, rock water.
Too little understanding, the balance tips from life.

I try to see the figure undivided, as if it were one life
and I could say, "Life!" and that would encompass
all. It only lets me know that it is breathing.
Times when I am acute—holding
a hand or standing alone lashed by my own winter—
that breath is felt, expressed by me.

So much
And not enough.
To see the universe whole I think I must awaken
Its blind eye.
In that eye my thought would melt into flame,
ever everywhere

Awe

Before the earliest words were etched
on bark or rock, papyrus, anything at all,
there was *awe*. It came from neither
lore nor law, but everyone knew it
when it came and knew it came from
deep inside. Say *wonder,* and you have
its edge, *appreciation* and you double
the gain (question and introspection.)
It's the kind of thought that hangs in air
above your head—like *beautiful, kind…*

Perspective

The carpenter's eye is on the plan.
He measures twice before he cuts
and throws the scrap away.
The concrete footing, all right angles,
is level as the mason's eye.
Stacked atop the grass nearby
a dozen isosceles tresses neat as pi—
even lying on their sides—wait
for the studs to rise. As neat as T's
the frame is tied by two-by-threes.
The carpenter stands back and eyes
the steady symmetry with pride.
He thinks it will stand squarely there
long after he and I have died.

Violets by the site lie flat
beneath a wayward two-by-six,
bent and rusted nails are strewn
among the trampled irises,
and the pansies were only annuals
anyway. I look to the rose-
tinted sky where clouds form elegant
shapes that quickly melt away.

The Wizard's Book

The grave old wizard knows that oceans move
in restless rhythms, power and grace that test
with treachery and buoyant hope, so like
the contrapuntal song of inconstant wind
and wave within the tides of human lives.

In this unquiet motion islands rise
where wind becomes enchanted song, where tides
from either side conspire to reconcile,
accept the magic circle love may weave.
This is where the sympathetic eye
sees all the world as natural and strange.
This need that fills the soul with wondrous wine
suspends all time, moves as oceans do
under the pull of the moon. And when we enter
at this place we too but *suffer a sea
change into something rich and strange.*

The wizard closed his magic book,
grave thoughts he called before his eyes,
and some forgiveness ere he dies.
And still, *Nothing of him that doth fade...*
for *Those are pearls that were his eyes.*
for *Those are pearls that were his eyes.*

Closing lines: Ariel, The Tempest; Act I, sc. ii

Song

The air is chill today.
Thin ice hides ashes under water,
years in a bed of leaves where
no life grows.

I think an old man will be
reclaimed in that black pool.
On every side the moving water
sings all summers into green
and helps redeem the voice
now only speaks of ice.

...reason is but choosing *

There's a tree on our street that yields
few leaves, sheds dead skin from
all the high limbs. There is rot within.
Woodpeckers pry its secret spaces.
Perhaps tomorrow if the wind picks up
it will fall. If it could think, perhaps
it would not wait.

The creek races in the spring, tumbles
over rock and sings. It has a mission,
to be moving all the way to the sea.
After the snows have run and springs
retreat beneath the hill each trickle
ends in a stagnant place where purpose
is only standing still.

The soul knows
neither wood nor water need reason,
being untried by blight of mind
or blinding pain.
Nature requires that they abide
among the lingering dead
when vital life has putrified.

---

*From "Areopagitica," a pamphlet published in 1644 by John Milton in opposition to the "Order of the Lords and Commons for the Regulating of Printing," issued by the Parliament of England in 1643. Reprinted with an introduction and commentary in Areopagitica, Sir Richard C. Webb, ed. Cambridge: University Press, 1918.

Paradox

In a moment
this thought arose:
all this time
these measured days
the numbered years
and passages
are suddenly

a single moment.

I am now contained
in this small thought
      and
It is already gone.

A shudder of fright,
not about death at all
but that life
is not merely swift
but has no time larger
than a moment
much too small
for a large design
no matter what gods
no matter sudden sight.

In His Eighty-first Year

What if a man bonds in family so deep
it seems ligaments in the sensory pits
of mind are sore with memory?

What if almost every subject of love
and thought and physical being are
simply (no, not simply) taken away?

What if the cause is self, serious harm
the half-aware man made, in half-blind
writhing half a life ago?

What if the prisoner has turned, made
each will a penance, worked some
recompense, understood and burned.

Too little matter: his life's an enemy.
There's a world gone mad.

November of An Old Professor

Through faded lens old eyes retrieve
Germanic vines that weave like Hell's
Dark light in lines of *Paradise Lost; but*
where did all those acolytes go, whose
eyes refreshed a wry, contemplative mind?
He still sees young lights gleaming
brown or blue to green upon the vine.

Why then, does he desire to resurrect
those weathered vines, to ply them with
his humbler fire, to teach the Golden
Issue of the wine, aged to its finest hour
with a weathered cask
bound in weathered brass?

Seed to seed to life conceiving,
life to life to life redeeming.

After reading Stanley Kunitz' "The Sea That Has No Ending"

Grief

Perhaps you have entered that infinite space
where only the ache seems real and the rest
like the hum of a distant machine. Voices
follow on padded feet and your smiles
are muffled replies to sympathetic eyes.

Gone, but felt nearby, like a shadow life
of nerves in an amputated leg, and you say,
"Where…?" but that returns you to your
space where only the ache remains, the
hollow center of grief. Even so, voices
reach you there and you answer, lovingly.

Something in you knows that morning comes
after the rites and heavy days are done
and the long bonds of love do not break
when twisted hard as this.

Cemetery Stones in Winter
(for Robert)

Snow gives them a postcard look,
                             serene, peaceful.
But we come there for one we know and love,
not for the poetry of snow.
A special presence of mind is what we carry
to that cold place, each one's presence, a
                                  communion.
We speak from a spirit within, and what is spoken
is familiar, of family, a presence that never melts.
We stand in a row and say the words together.

As we leave we see again the postcard scene,
silent coexistence with others' lives, others' losses
among cold stones' community.

Family
(for Eleanor)

All through the ice of winter she lay
fragile and light as a Meissen figurine
wrapped within her family's embrace,
her bright chemise a slash of springtime
color amid pale sheets, dark eyes
alive when one of her own came in.

Mother of seven, grandmother of thirteen,
she didn't want to leave a one of these—
not now, not even from this breathless bed
where every day and every night she
struggled for a little air, waiting for one
of her own to appear at the bedroom door.

Years before, the third of seven died, and
everyone knew he never left her grieving eyes;
and every other child, in their own light,
she held them in her eyes as if her sight—
stronger than all the mistakes that they
could make—would bring them safely home.

And there they came, loving sons and daughters
in attendance every day. "Whatever she wants
is what we'll do;" and round the clock and
turn by turn she never was alone at home,
and the strength was in their eyes this time
and she relied on their determined care.

Nobody's arms are stronger than time.
Hands that stroked her hair, and lips that
kissed her in the night, they always knew
their energy could not diminish dying;
each touch was only to delay the leaving, and
every kiss a godspeed with the lips and grieving.

Conversation

Around the burnished box
the mourners stand
composed as snow.

The simple measure of the box,
a last mute grace
poised to drop.

Someone's prayers hum in the
empty places

where each one's speech is dumb.

Burial Day

Dry words spin in wind above your grave
this cold November day: sermons
and the soft talk of kin—
silence burdened words.
You give them no reply,
and they hear you, yes they do.

Cemetery Stones

From the road, row on row,
ordinary stones speak each regret
a few feet up to a grey afternoon.
A path is trampled down the lane
from where five cars, a hearse, a
shining black limo, stand idle.
There's a backhoe off to one side
where two men wait to finish a day.

The grievers, respectful sorrow
starched into each face, file to a grave.
We listen to the universal prayers;
then, single file, each one drops
a flower on the box; wordless, they
file away, having memorized the day.
One lingers to touch the box.

Inside the efficient limousine
mourners stare across stones
seeking something that remains

Forest Hills Cemetery
(for Robert)

For these a world is laid to rest; yet in our time
and mind, we know them still. Their lives,
like ours, distinct, unique, embody change.
Nor do they cease in transformation outside time.
We see a greening season; in their arc of change
they join a supple universe in its vast inbreathing.

Transformation moves all forms of life, mute
acceptance of what is, wordless energy ever
becoming, never the same. Look within trans-
formation in your energy of memory and
mind: you see that great grey beech near the
cemetery gate? At first you saw sun-dappled
green, then entered under branches where their
dark made mystery a joyful light. Your play of
mind became a transformation.

Where does such mystery go? Like a dream
it lingers in time, in death follows the body
where every energy flows. You who mourn
are part of this, being here. It's not a distant
place or god you seek to know in the weight
of grief. It's a life beneath that tree, temporal
touch of dream's eternity.

There's a place in the mind tuned to a universe
that harbors everything: mystery and harmony,
perhaps the call of strings, that their vibrations
move in every center. Whatever it may be, we
are there, learning to listen, to try to see a weave

of reality that conceives our being. Like Indra's jeweled net* that spans our universe, each weave connected to all others, in each center every knot contains a crystal gem that reflects, receives, enjoins in every other.

A matter of belief or a matter of an endless search, how does it matter? For one beside a grave a place inside is full of sorrow, regrets, mind inquires after signs. This too is our reality; it exists in love's inner space which we enter to become another who feels
   in time all centers of eternity.

---

*Indra's net: Metaphor from The Flower Ornament Scripture in Mahāyāna Buddhism.

In a Graveyard

I came upon a low stone,
innocent and artless as
a lone man's sigh.
Side by side two hearts were put
as simple as a valentine,
and under these, "Forever" cut
to tell her how he pined.

The traffic of the world goes by,
how is it he still sighs,
and years on years still holds her love
his ageless steadfast prize?
The traffic of the world goes by,
all things on motion thrive;
the stillness in a secret heart
keeps her, and him, alive.

Written for an elderly man who asked me to check his wife's grave as I ran through the cemetery on my daily exercise.

Old Men on Monday

The Monday morning they sit in sun
outside Panera's bread and coffee shop,
four or five wise (wizened, wry) old
friends who keep their cups to go inside
for seconds, free, perhaps to hit the john.
They still rely on GI stories, sports of course,
kids and wives. Sport debates are
decibels above the rest, the cost of error
being more and less. Old events take
doughy shape, repetitious deceptions
stiffen like jam in cellars of memory.
Some memories lose the body, even if
a face remains (the fading Cheshire cat
who's never named.) People get revised.
Some ordinary guy becomes a play,
plot uncertain, but the character unwinds:
crazy guy—like the night he drank a fifth
of (name your brand) and died.
"I consoled his wife that night."
"Reminds me of the time…" and so it goes.
What of times which could not speak?
Those wait for night, a time alone with urns
and promises, deceits that bring a shame,
moments of some pride, a little fame,
other delights that only you and I do whisper
in our beds. Thus, another Monday morning
drifts away. Patience then, and maybe one
at home who, day by day, restrains a heavy sky.

Oh, Them Golden Years

When did you start to think, my love,
of regularity? where in all our vows
was rectal pain? where the wonder
at the mirror viewing sad decay,
chins beneath the layered grins and
wrinkles no massaging could delay?

Consider all the compensations:
half price fares and meals on wheels,
politicians feigned respect
and our association's deals.

AARP, of thee we sing,
and buy your health insurance,
supplemental vitamins
and pills to give endurance,
travel ads, incontinence pads
and battery driven carts,
advice on keeping youthful ways
for old decrepit farts.

The New Old Old

We are aware we have lost veneration,
the place by the hearth where the wisdom
is told; we've traded all that for a piece of
the action, life that is lengthy, lively and bold.

We're aware of neutrons, mesons, quarks,
gravity's force in the warp of space,
even the riddle of Schrodinger's cat;
that, and the dowry of toxic waste.

We're aware of technology, instant awareness,
images heaped to defeat contemplation,
thought that is shattered to multiply sight
to be dreamed in hours of restless night.

We're aware of hatred, misery, war
in cities we never have seen, and we know
where the first born's first born sleeps
among other dead in the scalding heat.

We're aware more than ever before
of potential for man to destroy and create
with weapons of greed and weapons of hate,
or imagination that sees beyond these.

And we are aware that the changes we see
never alter our need for those intimate feelings,
sharing our lives in our love and our pain,
the music that echoes again and again.

Lucinda

Days pass in dinner, medication,
what interruption the next cart brings.
Night is a raft on a dark sea. I rarely
sleep, listening to the restless ones, women
who have nothing new to dream,
hearing those who sleep and turn and cry,
disheveled men who shuffle in confusion
to my still lonely room, listening
for one secret minute when pure
silence strikes sudden peace.
I wonder am I lucky to be sane;
clear in mind and frail in all my bones,
I have never been so alone
listening.

For a 92-year old nursing home resident.

Naming in the Wards

Some think it's funny I talk to
empty air. I don't, of course,
though I'm very sick and feel
abandoned, which I'd say may be
the same. So many years locked
where all say I am crazy, not
my name, my name...

The way it is explained, I'm
diagnosed as *HeesAThis*, *HeesAThat*;
then, passing through a stage, they
say how I behaved. *"Acted out,"*
they say. But no applause not for
my name, my name...

Recovery is slow. *Never* seems the day.
Today our group will do how faces
can be made in papier mache. We are
assured they may be named, though
it's safer to refuse in papier mache
my name, my name.

On Becoming Blind

I fear a way of life is about to disappear.
Naturally. I'll still see as many colors
as mind allows, many shapes of day,
from latitudes of memory, hundreds
of fully expressive faces, and more
who populate the edges of my history
and theirs. Many dark inventions will
find expressive places. All this has
the shapes of adventure consciously
designed in separate psychic places.

So this: still using a computer screen,
still peeking to find a comma to say,
not quite enough, my friend,,,it is, says
that I'm ready now (there's an evasion)
to carry on with the best good cheer I
now believe is real. We'll see.

Johnny Lost His "Mister"

The name's John Doe. Call me Johnny,
a sick old man in hospital clothes.
I lost my socks and dungarees,
lost my buttons—feel the breeze,
even lost my "Mister" here.
but here's the loss that chiefly gnaws,
I've lost my manly underdrawers.
I'd complain, but they don't heed,
and smirk when you are cheeky.
If that's the case, I want to know,
why do they want my cheeks to show?

I take their pills and needles easy,
pasty meals, electric bed;
sick or well, I'm ready to be,
but doc, you know
what hurts the most?
Losing me.

Dementia

I am aware
of my decay,
the dying eyes of memory
that day you came to visit me.

I am aware
of the space within,
the mind that tries.
Will I be gone before I die?
I, familiar stranger at the door,
come and go, unexpected guest.
Slower than I like, I slip away.

Written following a visit to a family member with dementia. Curt's own experience with memory loss began many years later.

Places in the Heart*
(for my Love)

I will not have you besieged by priests
or asked to deny the love that had no creed.
Let others drag love and pain into the book
where only logic and dogma prevail—sentiments
dispensed like incense, unfeeling form,
graceless in the spaceless dimension of loss.

The human heart
embraces the entrance of pain so large
no other place can let it in.

Though I delight in all your happiness and joy
that reaches everywhere, I would not be so mean
to think your heart will not bear pain when I am gone.
Love, I know that you will have me there,
and that is enough eternity for me.

---

* "There are places in the heart which do not yet exist, and into which we enter suffering in order that they may have existence." –Leon Bloy

The Poet Donates His Body to a Medical School

An anatomic gift, a bit of thrift, Horatio,
my wedded parts disjoined to grace
an antiseptic table, to give an earnest
acolyte a hands-on try to learn (sans my
undeserved complaints) hidden signs
of brief humanity's interior design.
There'll be no ghost to haunt the stage,
no sentient threat or plea for sympathy.
And when my bones teach nothing new,
in memory my too too disembodied self
(except within the urn upon the shelf)
will now and then appear in unintended
stealth—perchance in some poor poet's
metered dream. He'll view what's left
and say, Alas, poor man, I knew his
brief tirades when he began to strut his
verse upon the stage. O God, how weary,
stale, flat—and most of all, unprofitable—
his too-too-heavy lines upon the page.

--Curt G. Curtin, patient poet

Le Chaim
(for Harvey Roazen)

Chaotic as squalls in a small boat,
your tangled lines ran dear through seas,
you, who anyway taught the green deeps
caught the green and willing apprentices
and me
in many attentive nets.

We drift on course for home
listening for echoes of ourselves,
something clean and clear and sure,
unutterably strange
as only love is. And loss.
Each enduring to be caught, to know again
that touch that ever swings—
it does still swing in the sea—the touch
untouched by hate or need or
the mean sting that hovers in little things.
The touch of you who rode the swing of the sea
so laughingly
so lovingly.

OTHER POETRY COLLECTIONS BY CURT CURTIN

<u>For Adults</u>
In Our Name. San Francisco, CA: Atticus Publishing, 2024.
Nature's Eclectic Designs. American Fork, UT: Kelsay Books, 2023.
Kerry Dancers. American Fork, UT: Kelsay Books, 2020.
For Art's Sake. American Fork, UT: Kelsay Books, 2019.

<u>For Children & Young Adults</u>
So Much Depends on Where You Live. American Fork, UT: Kelsay Books, 2022.
Why Trees Sneeze and Other Mysteries. American Fork, UT: Kelsay Books, 2021.

<u>Chapbooks</u>
Embers Carried Across a River in a Gourd, 2015
Elusive Music, 2005
Pacing the Floor, 1979

For more information, including audio-recordings of many poems in Curt's voice, please visit
www.curtcurtinpoet.com.

www.ingramcontent.com/pod-product-compliance
Lightning Source LLC
LaVergne TN
LVHW041851070526
838199LV00045BB/1550